101

THINGS EVERY MASTER NEEDS TO KNOW

FUNNY MASTERS DEGREE GIFT

101 Things Every Master Needs To Know

Funny Masters Degree Gift

Copyright©2024 by Davis Stamp

Congratulations on Your
Master's Degree.

You Are Master Degree.

Now You Need to Know
How to Prepare for Next
Level

No matter if you want a career
in science or want to make a
million dollars (or both)

ARE

YOU

READY?

3

2

But firstly. Remember.
The people who gave you
this book:

Love you

Believe in you

Are proud of you

They say you are
unstoppable!

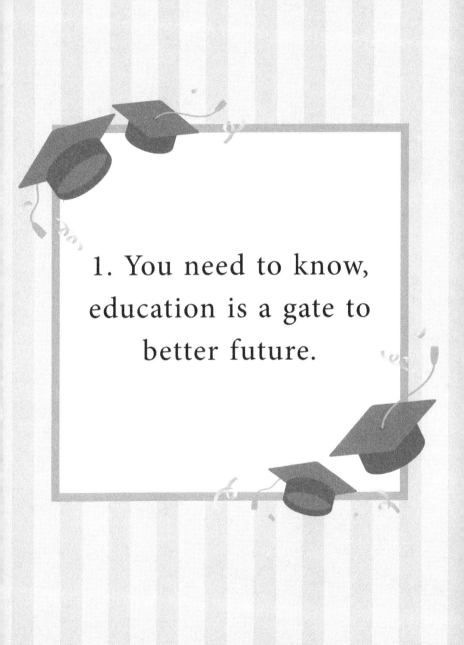

1. You need to know, education is a gate to better future.

2. You need to know. Now you can finally start getting paid to work rather than having to pay to do it.

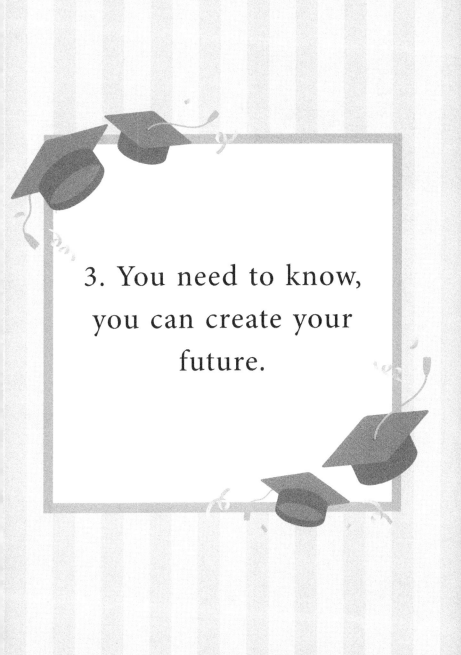

3. You need to know,
you can create your
future.

4. You need to remember, don't achieve people dreams, achieve your goals.

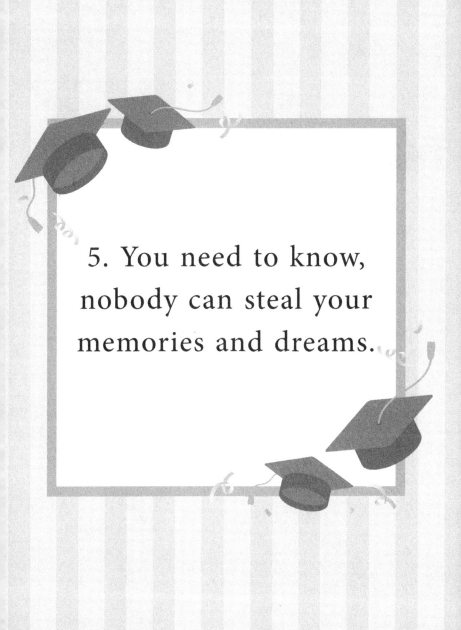

5. You need to know, nobody can steal your memories and dreams.

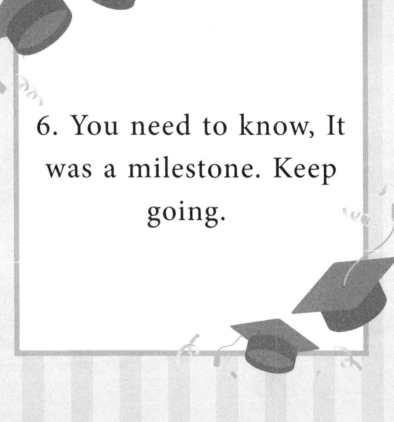

6. You need to know, It was a milestone. Keep going.

7. You need to know, it wouldn't be possible without the coffee.

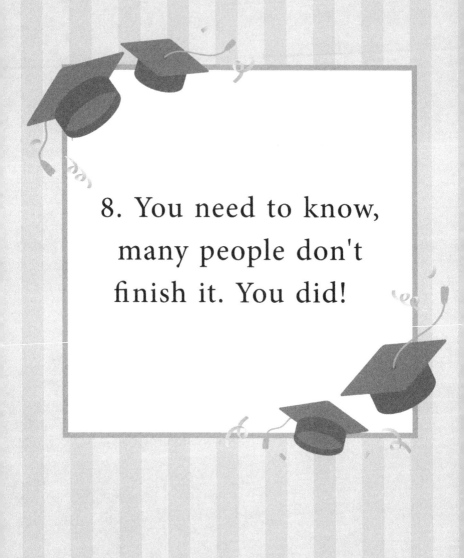

8. You need to know, many people don't finish it. You did!

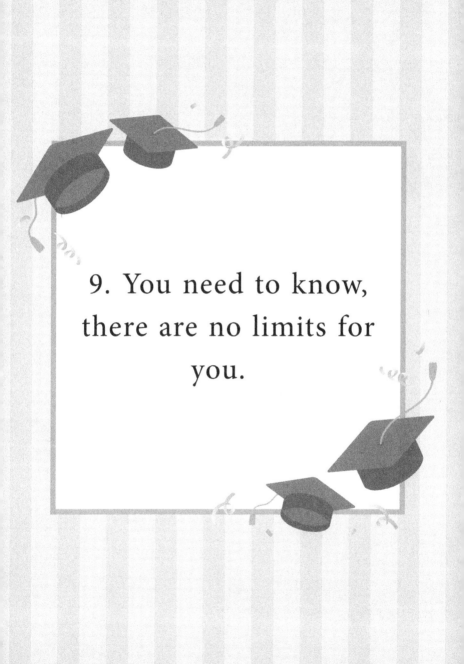

9. You need to know, there are no limits for you.

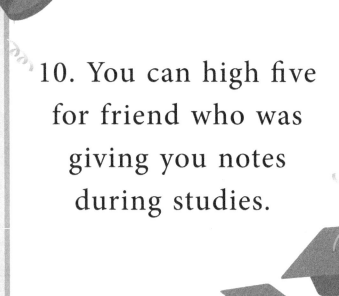

10. You can high five for friend who was giving you notes during studies.

11. You need to know,
you are the best one
who can play your role.

12. You need to hide your diploma. Just in case they try to take it back.

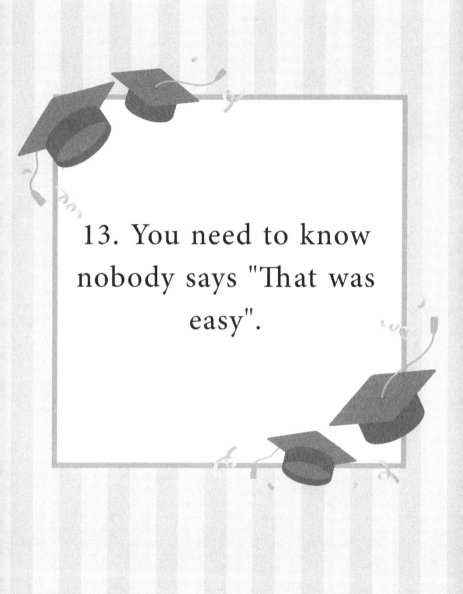

13. You need to know nobody says "That was easy".

14. You need to know, today it is first day your parents start collecting interest.

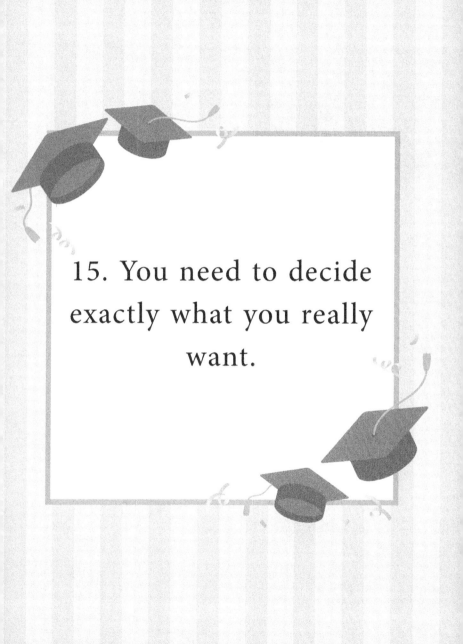

15. You need to decide exactly what you really want.

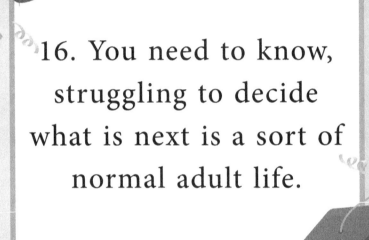

16. You need to know, struggling to decide what is next is a sort of normal adult life.

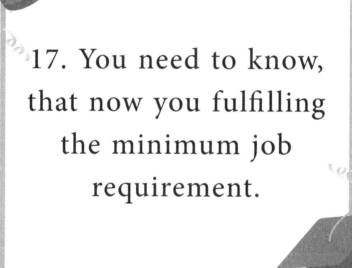

17. You need to know, that now you fulfilling the minimum job requirement.

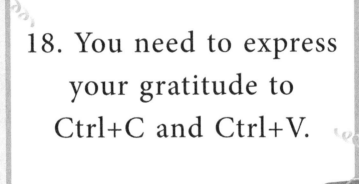

18. You need to express
your gratitude to
Ctrl+C and Ctrl+V.

19. You need to know, nobody notices what you are able to do until you do that.

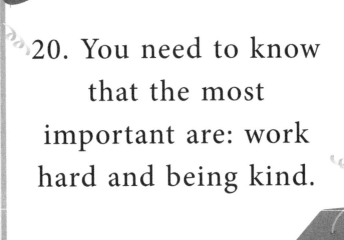

20. You need to know that the most important are: work hard and being kind.

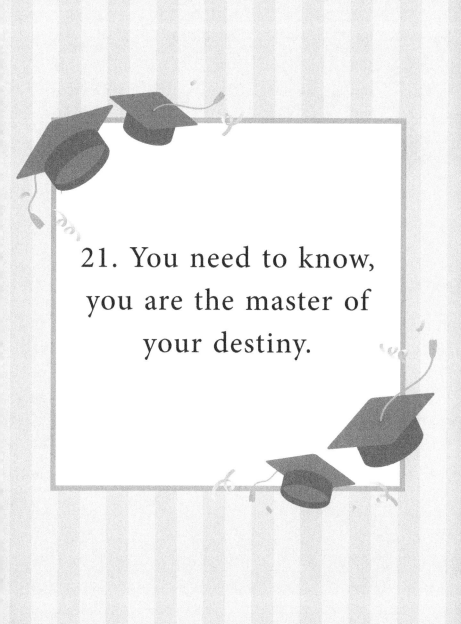

21. You need to know, you are the master of your destiny.

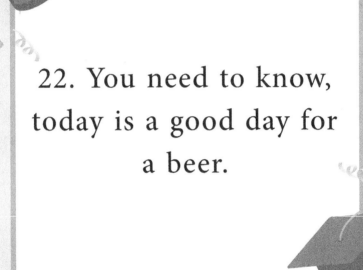

22. You need to know, today is a good day for a beer.

23. You need to know that it is one degree hotter in the places you are.

24. You need to know, in a few years, your haters will ask if you're hiring.

25. You need to know, the internet is your best friend at work as well.

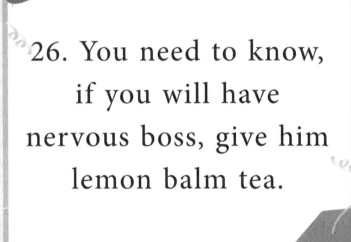

26. You need to know, if you will have nervous boss, give him lemon balm tea.

27. You need to know, today you don't need to thinking about student loan.

28. You need to question your leaders. But don't ask too difficult questions, because their heads will explode.

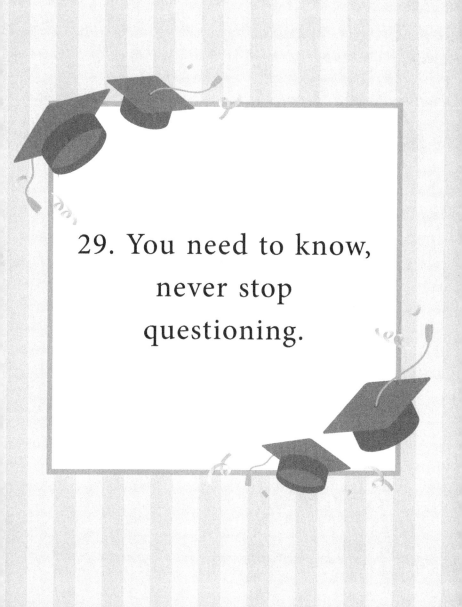

29. You need to know,
never stop
questioning.

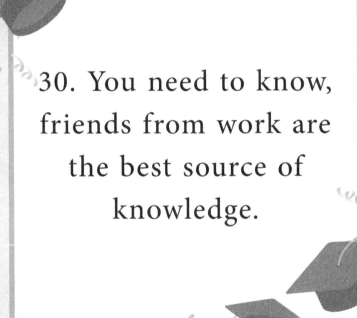

30. You need to know,
friends from work are
the best source of
knowledge.

31. You need to know that the hard work has just begun! (I want to hear about you in forbes magazine).

32. You need to know, that future is connected with what you do today. Take it easy, finish that beer.

33. You need to know, if nobody knows what you are doing, you aren't doing it wrong.

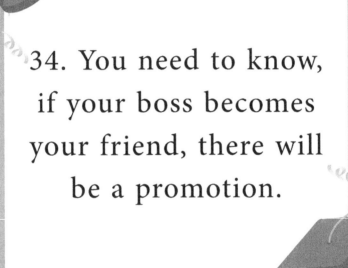

34. You need to know, if your boss becomes your friend, there will be a promotion.

35. You need to know, you can use your Cap and gown to make it a robe.

36. You need to know,
if it would be easy,
everybody would do
it.

37. You need to know,
If your family is
proud of you, this is
the best time to ask
for money.

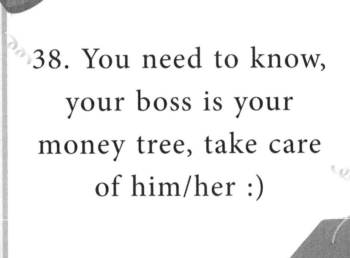

38. You need to know, your boss is your money tree, take care of him/her :)

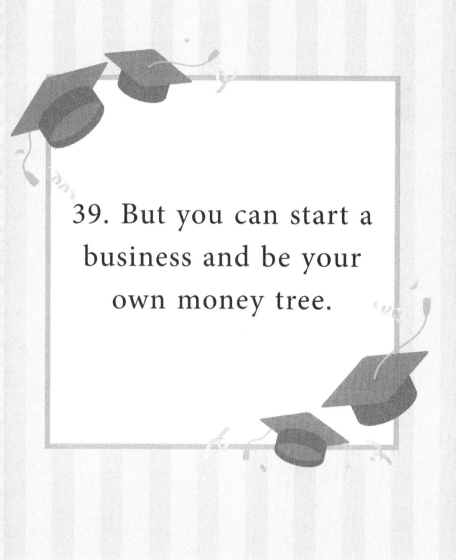

39. But you can start a
business and be your
own money tree.

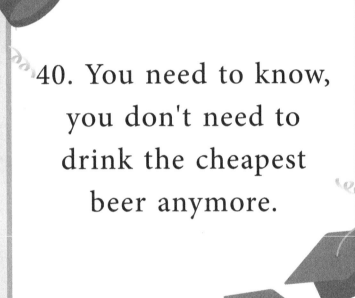

40. You need to know, you don't need to drink the cheapest beer anymore.

41. You need to know, there was no coincidence in your success.

42. You need to know, nobody is interested how many times you fail, you need only one big win to shocked up the world.

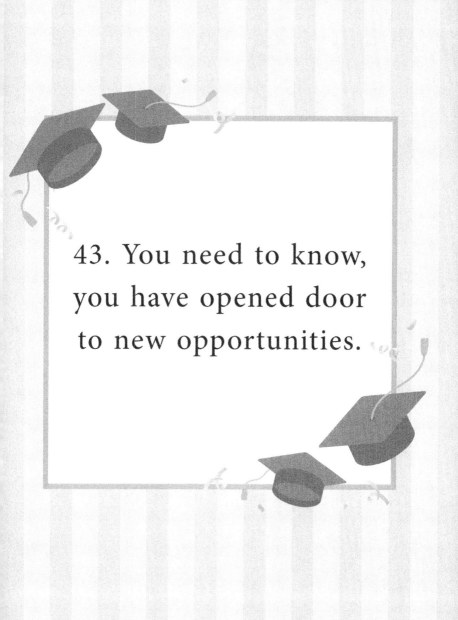

43. You need to know,
you have opened door
to new opportunities.

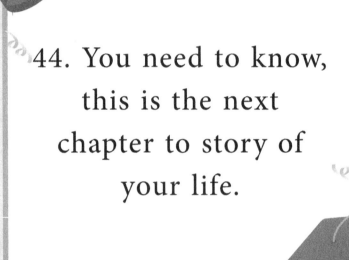

44. You need to know, this is the next chapter to story of your life.

45. You need to know. Get enough sleep, work hard and smart and you will be successful.

46. You need to know,
if you ever fail,
remember that better
days will come.

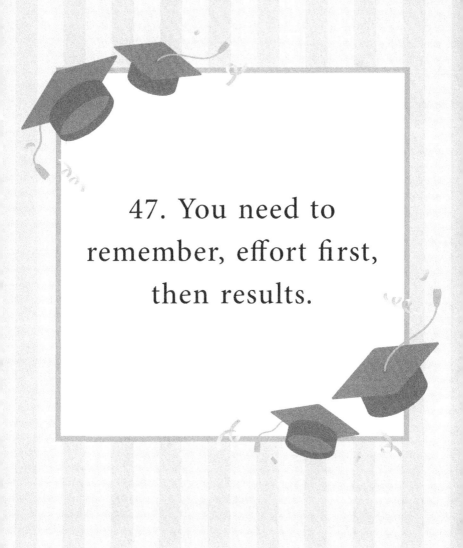

47. You need to remember, effort first, then results.

48. You need to know, now you will have money to develop your passion.

49. You need to know, swearing helps sometimes.

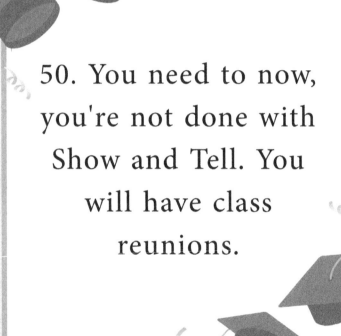

50. You need to now, you're not done with Show and Tell. You will have class reunions.

51. You need to know, learning doesn't stop just because you received a diploma.

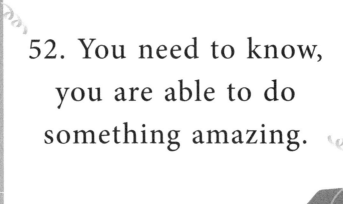

52. You need to know,
you are able to do
something amazing.

53. You need to know,
now you can read
books that you really
like.

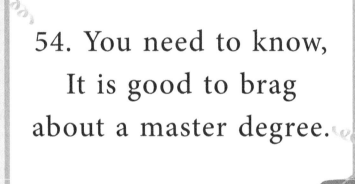

54. You need to know,
It is good to brag
about a master degree.

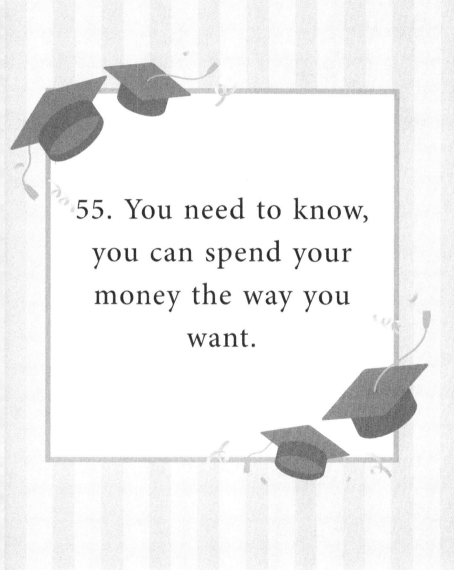

55. You need to know, you can spend your money the way you want.

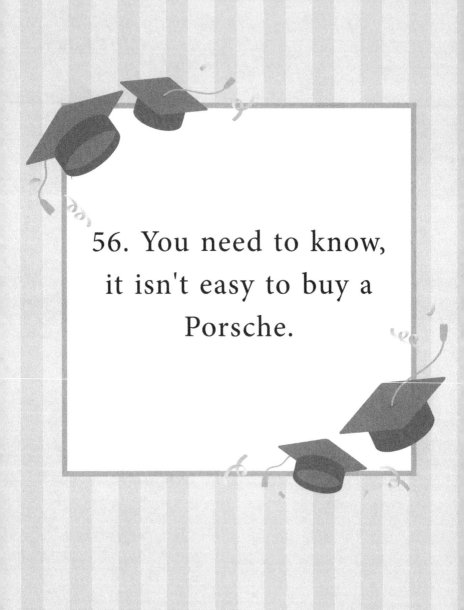

56. You need to know, it isn't easy to buy a Porsche.

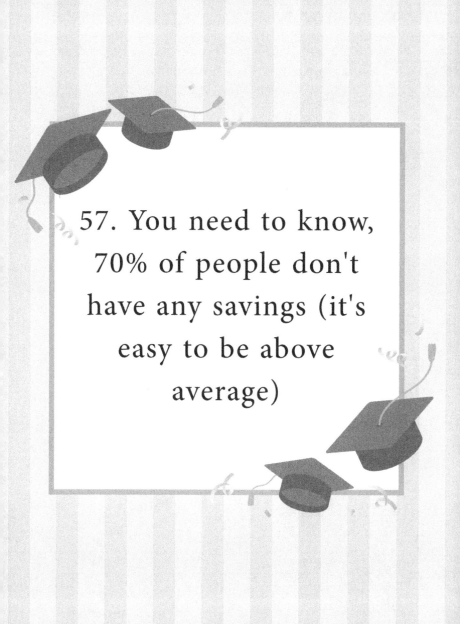

57. You need to know, 70% of people don't have any savings (it's easy to be above average)

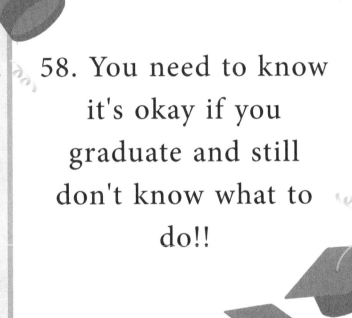

58. You need to know it's okay if you graduate and still don't know what to do!!

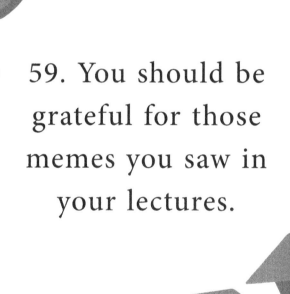

59. You should be grateful for those memes you saw in your lectures.

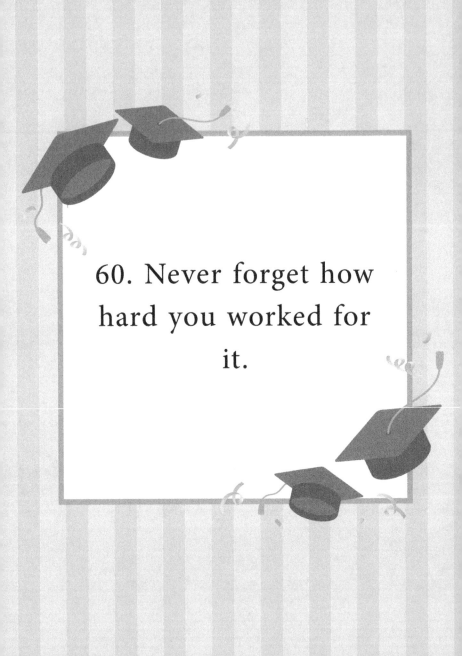

60. Never forget how hard you worked for it.

61. You need to know, we don't need magicians, we need masters.

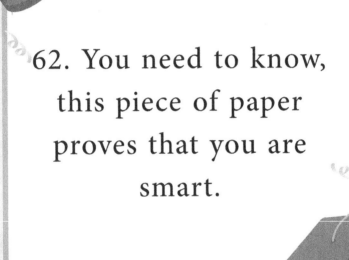

62. You need to know, this piece of paper proves that you are smart.

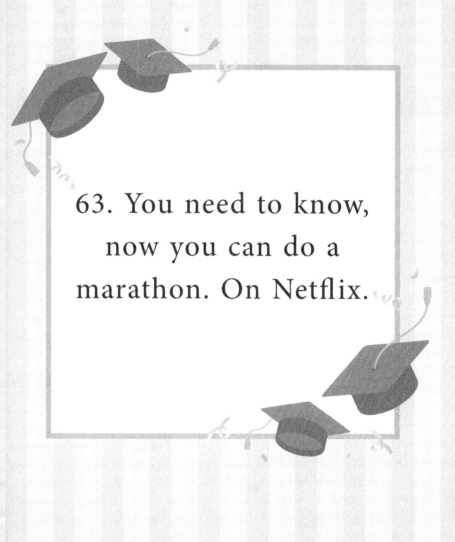

63. You need to know, now you can do a marathon. On Netflix.

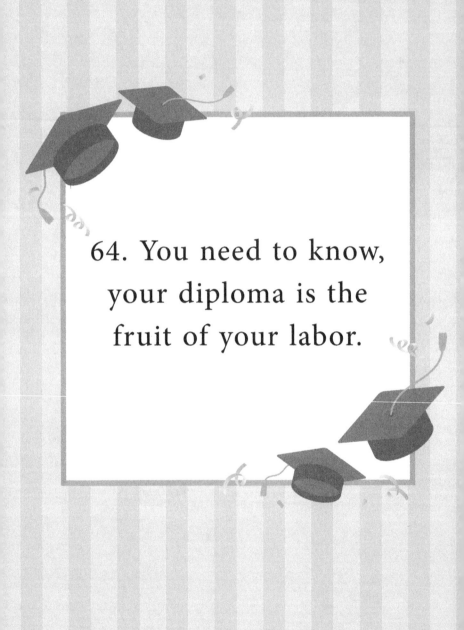

64. You need to know, your diploma is the fruit of your labor.

65. You need to know it's time for experience, then money, then you can share your experiences.

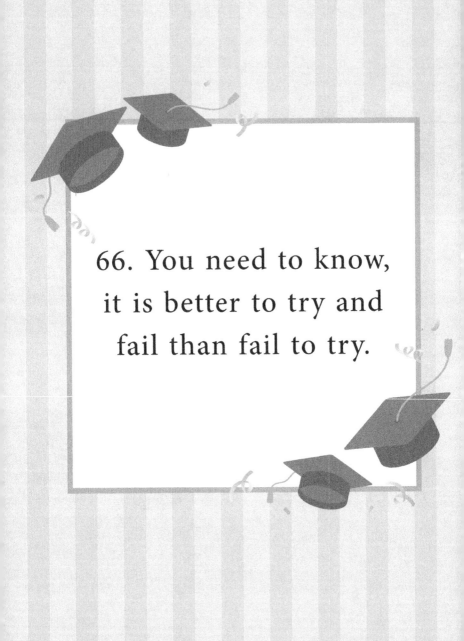

66. You need to know, it is better to try and fail than fail to try.

67. You need to know, in work phrase "the dog ate my report" may not work.

68. You need to know, you can't sleep at work after the party.

69. You need to know that you can easily find a better boss which was more difficult with a university lecturer.

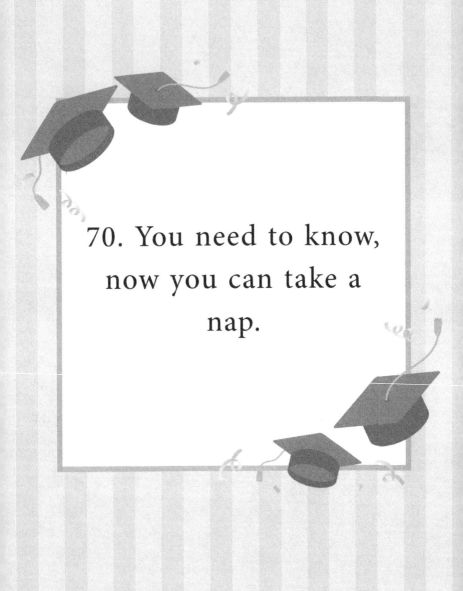

70. You need to know, now you can take a nap.

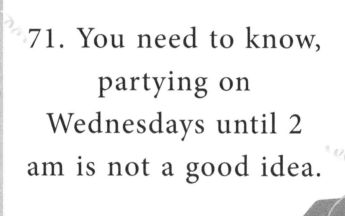

71. You need to know, partying on Wednesdays until 2 am is not a good idea.

72. You need to know, unlike college, now people over 50 can be your friends.

73. You need to know, you're pretty smart... You proved something everyone knows about you.

74. You need to remember the old true, aim for the moon because even if you miss, you'll find yourself among the stars.

75. You need to know, that your parents or other elders graduated without Google and Wikipedia.

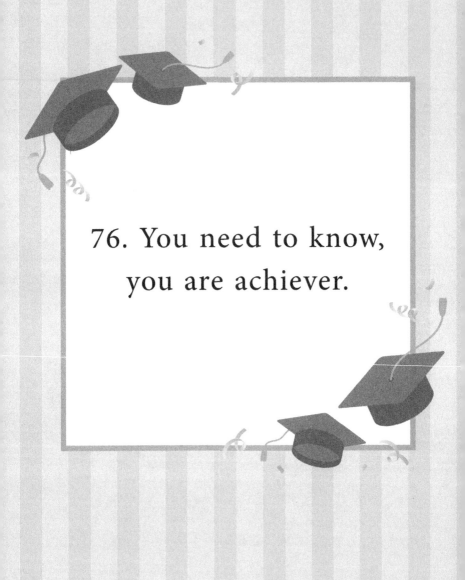

76. You need to know,
you are achiever.

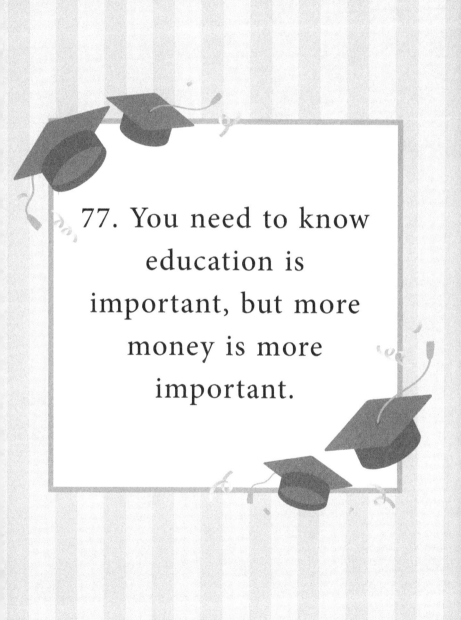

77. You need to know education is important, but more money is more important.

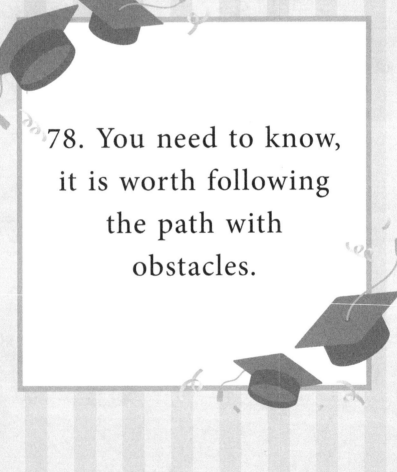

78. You need to know, it is worth following the path with obstacles.

79. You need to know,
we can't wait to see
where life will take
you next.

80. You should be glad that you could spend those times and money for this piece of paper.

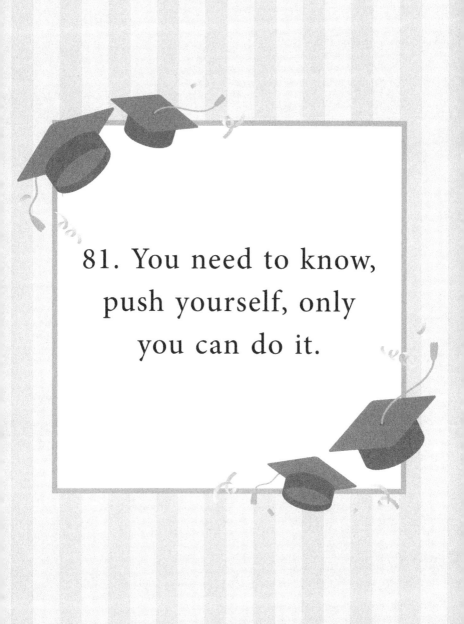

81. You need to know,
push yourself, only
you can do it.

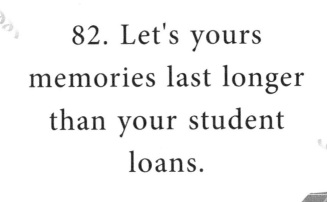

82. Let's yours memories last longer than your student loans.

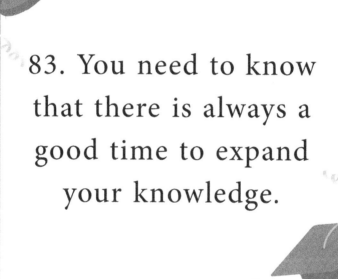

83. You need to know that there is always a good time to expand your knowledge.

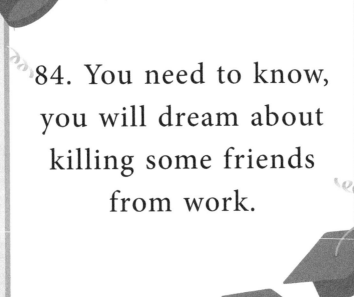

84. You need to know, you will dream about killing some friends from work.

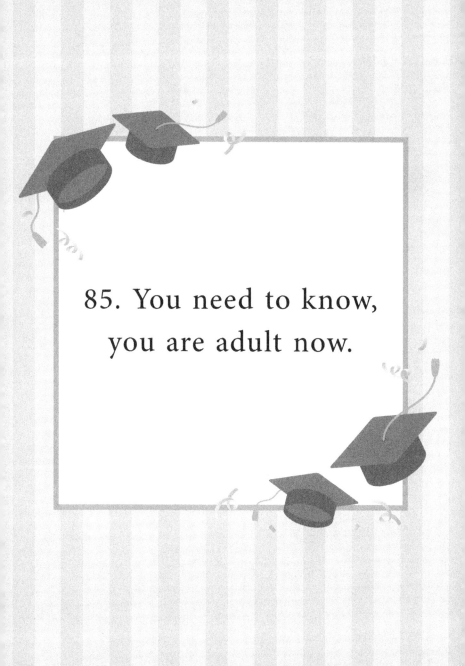

85. You need to know,
you are adult now.

86. You need to know, at work you can use your experience in writing ununderstandable and complicated reports.

87. You need to know,
you can use the ctrl+c
ctrl+v method in your
future work.

88. You need to know when your peers rested, you worked hard, and now you can say "I did it".

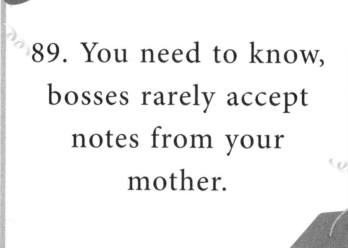

89. You need to know, bosses rarely accept notes from your mother.

90. You need to know, if you have learned enough to be able to read your diploma, everything is fine.

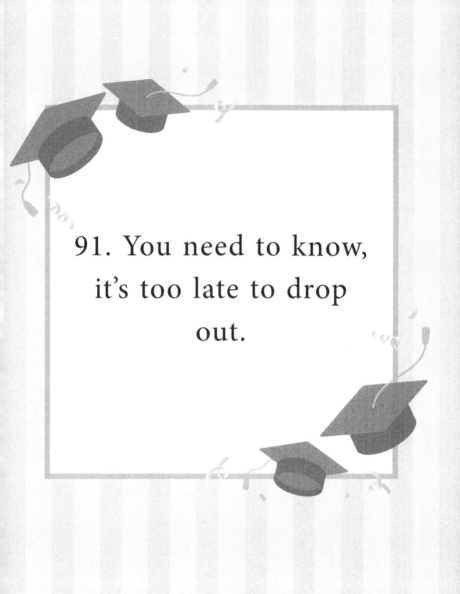

91. You need to know, it's too late to drop out.

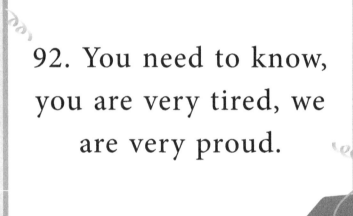

92. You need to know, you are very tired, we are very proud.

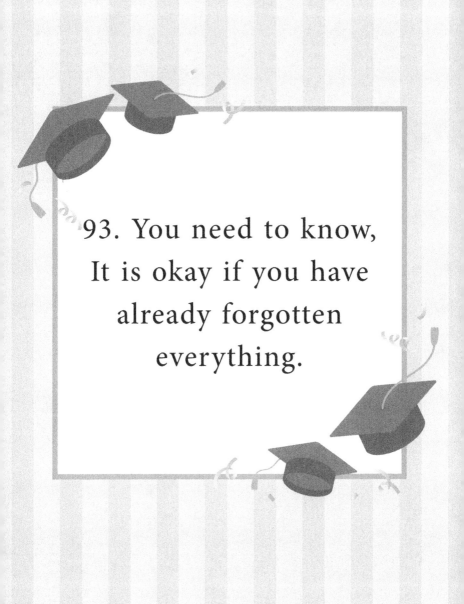

93. You need to know,
It is okay if you have
already forgotten
everything.

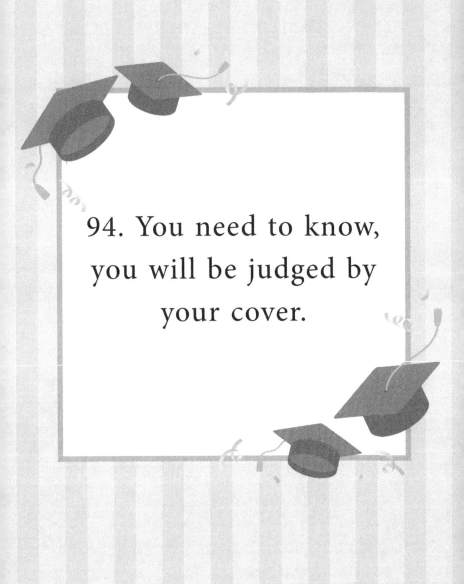

94. You need to know, you will be judged by your cover.

95. You need to know, thesis defense was difficult? Wait for your first speech to the company's management.

96. You need to know, fact that you were champion in beer pong won't make impression during job interview.

97. You need to know, now you have two mothers, your real one and your (diplo)ma.

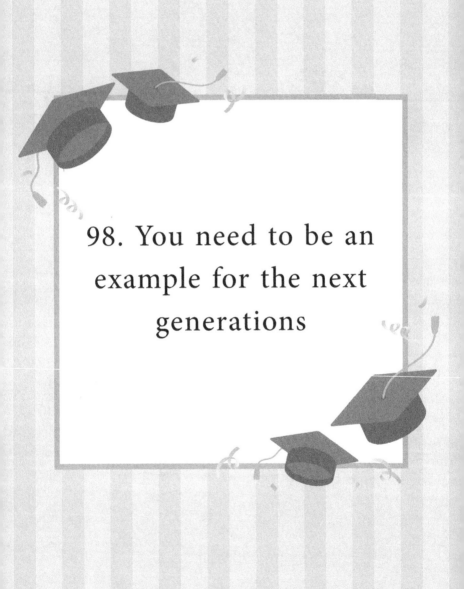

98. You need to be an example for the next generations

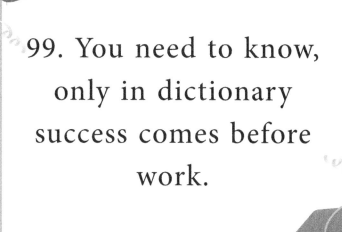

99. You need to know, only in dictionary success comes before work.

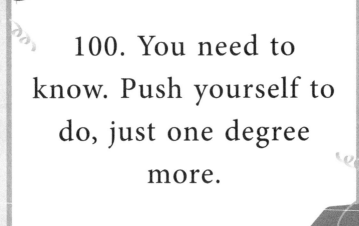

100. You need to know. Push yourself to do, just one degree more.

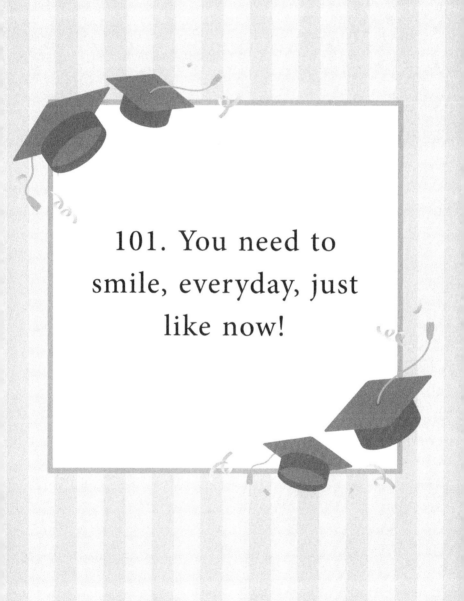

101. You need to smile, everyday, just like now!

Made in the USA
Middletown, DE
30 May 2025

76313189R00066